(DADDY! CAN I TAKE JESUS HOME?)

It's Christmas eve, Betty and her dad are out looking for a Christmas tree.

They came upon a sad scene where homeless people were sleeping in cardboard boxes and eating out of garbage cans. A deep sadness came upon their faces. Betty asked "Daddy, are we in Bethleham?" No child we are not.

They kept on walking and passed by a bridge where they could hear the cries of the sick and homeless. They were coughing and burning trash to keep themselves warm. Betty said " are we in Bethleham now! Daddy!

No why do you ask again? Well in the Bible, Bethleham is in the desert, and we are in the desert. " Child", said her father, there is homeless people everywhere, and we are not in Bethleham.

Why do we have homeless people daddy? Why? Is it becuase they don't believe in Jesus? No ! Those people use to have homes too before they lost there jobs.

Betty pulled on her dads coat and said, "daddy, that makes me very sad. Tonight after Jesus is born again, there will be no more homeless people, right daddy?" I hope so my child, I hope so."

Betty said, " I will ask for a miracle tonight when I say my prayers." Daddy tomorrow can we give some of our Christmas dinner to the homeless? Betty, I am not a rich man. I cannot feed them all."

But daddy, in the Bible it says we are to share aren't we? Yes child. We are, We shall see tomorrow what we can do. For now let us find a Christmas tree.

Betty felt happy. She looked up to the sky and said "Daddy do stars fall down?" Yes they do child sometimes.

Then there it was. A beautiful Christmas tree and in the bushes something was shining on the ground. Daddy, daddy, now we are in Bethleham, we are, we are.

Why do you keep on saying things like that my child? Well there was a bright star over where Jesus was born and there it is. There is a full moon tonight and it is shining on a old garbage can. That's all it is.

No Daddy, no. Jesus is born again. Right there in the garbage can. Look daddy, look how beautiful He is.

There it was in a tipped over garbage can. A baby covered with a old coat. Wrapped around Him a stray cat and dog keeping Him warm. Oh my God, said her dad, it is a baby.

I told you daddy. Jesus is born again. The father picked up the baby in his arms. Tears running down his face. Betty was jumping with joy. Daddy, daddy, can I keep Jesus. Daddy, daddy can I take Jesus home?

I will pray with Him to take care of all the homeless people. Look daddy over here. A gold box. The little girl picked up the Christmas tree and the box. The father picked up the baby and they went home.

They kept the baby warm in there home and in their hearts. There was a million dollars in the box. The father was rich. Betty still thinks the abandoned baby is Jesus.

The father took care of the homeless in his little town.

The money remained a mystery.

Betty's parents always help the poor . She help out also by baking fresh bread for them too.

And Betty never forgot her promise to pray for the homeless each and every night.

Betty's parents went out and bought new clothes for all the homeless.

Betty's father Also got them new places to live with running water.

He also got them warm beds and blankets too. With nice bathroom.

Her parents filled the cupboards with lots of food and clean running water to drink.

They love the baby so much they adopted him. Betty still calls him Jesus.

Betty kept the stray cat and dog. You see if you truly believe with all your heart and soul, miracles do come true.

Story was written and illustrated by:

Flossie Langdon Ward

About the author:

Flossie is 88 years old and was born in Ontario, Canada in October of 1927.

Published in agreement with:

Createspace Inc.

Copyrighted 2015

                                                  Merry Christmas

                                                  God Bless

www.ingramcontent.com/pod-product-compliance
Lightning Source LLC
Chambersburg PA
CBHW041552220426
43666CB00002B/50